Abba Father

Abba Father

DISCOVERING THE FATHERS LOVE

- DEVOTIONAL -

by Pola Fanous

ST SHENOUDA PRESS
SYDNEY, AUSTRALIA
2021

ABBA FATHER
Discovering the Fathers Love

Pola Fanous

COPYRIGHT © 2021
St. Shenouda Press

All rights reserved. Except for brief quotations in critical publications or reviews, no part of this book may be reproduced in any manner without prior written permission from the publisher.

ST SHENOUDA PRESS
8419 Putty Rd,
Putty, NSW, 2330
Sydney, Australia

www.stshenoudapress.com

ISBN 13: 978-0-6488658-9-6

All scripture quotations, unless otherwise indicated, are taken from the New King James Version®. Copyright © 1982 by Thomas Nelson, Inc. Used by permission. All rights reserved.

Acknowledgements

I would like to extend a special thank you to St Shenouda Press for allowing me this blessed platform and giving me an opportunity to glorify God with His gifts. To my father of confession, Fr Karas, without whose guidance I would have nothing to say at all. To Ruth Roffael for patiently revising this work, editing my bad grammar and helping me both understand myself better and be understood better. To my wise brother, Arsany for his counsel in tough times. To my wonderful Mama, Marsiel, for empowering me at my worst and celebrating me at my best. To my captivating fiancé, Alexandra, when I found you, I found love, and when I found love, I found God.

Introduction

Dearly beloved readers of this book – welcome! Wherever you are in this world and on your journey towards Christ, I want to assure you that Hope is never far from you; Jesus is always close. If you turn to Him in your simple heart, you will always find Him there, waiting with a smile. I have tried to write this book with theological accuracy as well as from my deep heart. If you find one sentence, one word, one idea in these pages that causes your heart to sing, then may God be glorified for His magnificent working, both in these words and in your Holy Heart which knows its Maker!

This book is a devotional style book. This means it is designed to be read slowly and thoughtfully, one chapter at a time – it is good for you to contemplate these words, to taste them and to try to live them. I advise you to read one chapter a day, after your morning prayer and bible reading. Hopefully, this will elevate your experience of God's Grace, and allow you to see Him across your day. I designed this book to inspire you from many angles – and so, each chapter includes a unique mixture of bible verses, Church Father quotes, the sayings of Saints and heart-stirring images.

To those of you who desire to seek Christ with all your heart, you are not alone on your journey! I too am seeking The Face of the Beloved and yearning to know Him as a friend, more each day. May God bless each person who reads these words with His holy joy, His perfect peace, His awe-inspiring love, His heavenly light, and every good and noble thing. Glory be God forever, Amen.

Part 1
Knowing God

To fall in love with God is the greatest romance;
to seek him the greatest adventure; to find
him, the greatest human achievement.
St Augustine

"Oh, taste and see that the Lord is good;
Blessed is the man who trusts in Him!"
PSALM 34:8

Abba Father

Undoubtedly, in Sunday School we all learned that God is our Father. When we were told this, some of us rejoiced and others grimaced – depending on how positively we viewed fathers as being. Fr. Anthony Messeh says that our painful experiences with our earthly fathers' cause many of us to believe that a father is fundamentally, "unpleasable and unreasonable, unstable and unable." Fr. Anthony reassures us that our Heavenly Father is nothing like that at all. God, our Father, is always close and always caring. When we reject Him, He seeks us. He is LOVE – and we are His children!

> "Behold what manner of love the Father has bestowed on us, that we should be called children of God! Therefore the world does not know us, because it did not know Him." – 1 John 3:1

If you have had a difficult experience with your earthly father, do not be discouraged. As a result of this, you have been blessed with a *special* relationship with God, who mercifully promises to be…

> "A father of the fatherless, a defender of widows, is God in His holy habitation." – Psalm 68:5

Abba Father

As Christians, baptised in the Church, we must always remember that God is *truly* our loving Father. Let us declare confidently with King David, unashamed and unafraid: we know *who* & *whose* we are!

> "… the Lord has said to Me, 'You are My Son, today I have begotten You.'" – Psalm 2:7

If you are reading this, I invite you to live in the comfort of God's generous invitation: to honour you as He did Jesus, with the perfect Fatherly love you have always sought, desired and prayed for!

> "And suddenly a voice came from heaven, saying, "This is My beloved Son, in whom I am well pleased." – Matthew 3:17

What does God's Fatherhood mean to us on a practical level? It means we are protected, watched over as a father watches over his son. It means we are provided for, that God cares for our littlest needs, cares, and wants! It means God encourages us constantly, like a father at his daughter's dance recital. Our Loving Father does this by sending to us moments of divine illumination, where we experience His Holy Joy. Besides this, God is responsible for replenishing our souls, minds, hearts, and bodies, just as a father is responsible for their child's wellbeing. God replenishes us joyfully and constantly through our regular partaking of the sacraments of Holy Communion and Confession.

Finally, God's Fatherhood also includes fatherly discipline. God loves us too much to leave us in misery, and so he lovingly guides us back home to goodness through correction and discipline.

> "My son, do not despise the chastening of the Lord, nor detest His correction; for whom the Lord loves He corrects, just as a father the son in whom he delights." – Proverbs 3:11-12

Part I / Abba Father

When God chisels away at the sinful parts of us, purifying us lovingly for our own sake, we must remember that we ought to surrender to His plans for us, for they are **ALWAYS** good for us!

Among the many privileges we receive as Children of God, is the *stamp* of God the Father Himself. Just as an Australian coin belongs to the British monarchy and has the image and likeness of Queen Elizabeth II stamped into it; you and I belong to heaven, and as such we have the image and likeness of God stamped into our very souls! By God's Grace, a loving Christian is a true icon of Jesus Christ.

> "There are two different coinages, so to speak, in circulation, God's and the world's, each with its own distinctive marking. Unbelievers carry the stamp of the world; while the faithful in love bear the stamp of God the Father, through Jesus Christ." – St Cyprian of Carthage

As Orthodox Christians, we must never forget the monumental importance of the Church in our Christian practice as well as to our journey to The Everlasting Joy. St Cyprian of Carthage writes, *"No one can have God for his Father, who has not the Church for his mother."* His words ring true, and as all children being raised in fullness, we too must be nurtured lovingly by both a father and a mother. Due to COVID-19, many of us have experienced being restricted from being nourished by the bosom of our beloved mother – the Church – and how unfortunate that is! As churches re-open, let us run with love into the hands of our Mother, for I assure you – this makes your Heavenly Father rejoice! Remember always, beloved, that God is not – as we often feel – cold, distant, angry, judgemental, or harsh. These are lies we project onto God based on our experiences with our earthly fathers. God is good! God is kind, generous, gentle, ever-close, ever-present, always loving, blessing, and nurturing you, for you are his beloved child! He loves you so much, that He in fact, lavishes you with gifts:

Abba Father

> *"Every good gift and every perfect gift is from above, and comes down from the Father of lights, with whom there is no variation or shadow of turning."* – James 1:17

What level of intimacy does God the Father seek with you? Infinite! When Jesus taught us to pray, He told us to address God as our father! *"In this manner, therefore, pray: Our Father in heaven..."* (Matthew 6:9). Elsewhere, Jesus called God: "Abba" – a word meaning 'papa', 'daddy' or 'baba'! God desires you to be so close to Him that you call Him 'Baba'! That is the level of intimacy that God wants to have with YOU! May His holy and perfect name be glorified everywhere always! When you next pray, imagine God holding His hands out towards you, welcoming you into His Kingdom of Peace. Let us recognise His love in the sweet, unconditional acceptance that our Father of Confession shows us when we repent for our sins. How blessed we are to have priests – the ambassadors of God's fatherly love, here, on earth. Let us conclude by exploring one final detail: the way that Jesus Christ our King – who is perfect, prayed and related to His Father in heaven: *"And He said, "Abba, Father, all things are possible for You. Take this cup away from Me; nevertheless, not what I will, but what You will.""* – Mark 14:36

> ### † thoughts †
> The next time you pray to Your Abba, will you say to Him: "Thy will be done"? Remember, my beloved, that when God is finally finished with us, we too – like a vase – will be perfected!

Even in His darkest hour, Christ called God 'Papa' and even in His darkest hour – Christ surrendered obediently to the will of His Loving Father. Let us also when we pray, and when we struggle, choose not to complain, but rather: to surrender in sweet humility to our God, declaring boldly, in faith:

Part 1 / Abba Father

"But now, O Lord, you are our Father; we are the clay, and You our potter; and all we are the work of Your hand." –
Isaiah 64:8

A Sheep in a Shepherd's Arms

"I am the good shepherd. The good shepherd gives His life for the sheep." – John 10:11

For me, the care of God has always been best embodied by the image of the Good Shepherd – Christ, with a staff in one arm, tenderly holding a frail sheep in His other arm. For years, this was my go-to icon. I would imagine myself being the small sheep in Jesus' arms, resting in perfect safety. What can harm the sheep who is always secure in the arms of His Shepherd? To better understand God's perfect care, let us explore together what the bible says about the Good Shepherd:

> *"What man of you, having a hundred sheep, if he loses one of them, does not leave the ninety-nine in the wilderness, and go after the one which is lost until he finds it? And when he has found it, he lays it on his shoulders, rejoicing. And when he comes home, he calls together his friends and neighbours, saying to them, 'Rejoice with me, for I have*

Abba Father

> *found my sheep which was lost!' I say to you that likewise there will be more joy in heaven over one sinner who repents than over ninety-nine just persons who need no repentance." – Luke 15:4-7*

Does it not strike your heart that Christ is willing to leave behind ninety-nine righteous sheep, to ensure that one lost sheep finds his way home!? Are you amazed at how He cares for you! When you go astray due to sin, God does not abandon you to your own devices, rather He hurries to you full of concern, for He knows that a small sheep without His protector is in terrible danger! Let us praise then, with St Andrew of Crete, that Christ may seek us when we are too blind to seek Him:

> *"Thou art the good Shepherd; seek me, Thy lamb, and neglect not me who have gone astray. Thou art my sweet Jesus, Thou art my Creator; in Thee, O Saviour, I shall be justified. I confess to Thee, O Saviour, I have sinned, I have sinned against Thee, but absolve and forgive me in Thy compassion."*

Why does He seek you so ardently, leaving the ninety-nine secure sheep to find you, the frail sheep? Because He loves you – yes YOU! And not with a normal love, but with a fiery love even unto death! *"Even so it is not the will of your Father who is in heaven that one of these little ones should perish."* (Matthew 18:14). After all, was Christ not crucified in Calvary that you may live eternally?

> **"Our Lord seeks to recall all humanity from death to life. For it was for us that he went to death, so that he might make us alive, these who had died. For he rejoiced even more over the hundredth sheep that was lost than over the ninety and nine." – Epiphanius Scholasticus**

Let us therefore hurry to seek the *Good* Shepherd, that we might implore Him to hold our weakness in His holy arms, to rescue us from this bitter wilderness, and to count us among His lively flock:

Part I / A Sheep in a Shepherd's Arms

"After Thee do I run, and Thy converse do I seek: that in me may be completed that number of a hundred, by means of a lost one which is found." – St. Jacob of Edessa

† thoughts †

A wonderful Orthodox icon of Christ the Good Shepherd. I adore this icon because of the tenderness present in Christ's face, the gratitude of the little sheep, and how perfectly they fit together... Truly, "You have made us for yourself, O Lord, and our heart is restless until it rests in you." – St. Augustine

If we are descended from The Good Shepherd, shouldn't we do more than bathe in blessings? Shouldn't we also share God's kindness with the world, and become – *albeit tiny* – good shepherds also? If you are reading this, I am certain you have a friend who has wandered into dangerous territory and become difficult to deal with, and whom for this reason, you have largely ignored.

We are sons and daughters of the Lord of Light, the Heavenly King, the Good Shepherd, and as we have seen our father do, we ought to do also: *"... the Son can do nothing of Himself, but what He sees the Father do; for whatever He does, the Son also does in like manner."* (John 5:19). When Christ comes, will He find us shepherding His flock, and tending to His sheep – the lame, the sick, the lost, the broken? I sure hope so, for I do not want to be like the hireling who flees in fear.

Abba Father

> "But a hireling, he who is not the shepherd, one who does not own the sheep, sees the wolf coming and leaves the sheep and flees; and the wolf catches the sheep and scatters them. The hireling flees because he is a hireling and does not care about the sheep." – John 10:12-14

As Christians, we ought always to learn from the perfect example of our Lord, Jesus Christ, who never gives up on us, abandons us, or leaves us to go astray or wander off the mountain's edge; but always in His supreme mercy, seeks us even when we do not seek Him… and thus has He revealed His love for us! St John Chrysostom, the golden-mouthed, paints this idea for us so wonderfully:

† *thoughts* †

On the left is a German mosaic of Christ the Good Shepherd depicting His sovereign safety! On the right is a Greek icon of Christ the Good Shepherd depicting his abundant, loving mercy… Truly, Christ extended a life-raft to us when He said:
"I am the good shepherd."
— John 10:11

Part 1 / A Sheep in a Shepherd's Arms

> *"If then God thus rejoices over the little one that is found, how do you despise them that are the objects of God's earnest care, when one ought to give up even one's very life for one of these little ones? But is he weak and mean? Therefore for this very cause most of all, one ought to do everything in order to preserve him. For even He Himself left the ninety and nine sheep, and went after this, and the safety of so many availed not to throw into the shade the loss of one."*

Here, I will leave you with three encouragements. I pray you know that you have a Good Shepherd, holding your fragility in His strong arms and pursuing your heart to the ends of the earth. I pray you know and feel and rest assured, that even in your blindness, you are guided by The One Who Sees. Finally, let us be good shepherds, in whatever little capacity we can, to our friends, our family, our colleagues, and to all of God's creatures, for we who truly love Him, must obey Him who said to us: "Tend My Sheep." (John 21:16). Please remember that all outreach ought to be done with love, humility and discernment – under the supervision of our Confession Fathers. In some situations, we must be self-aware enough to acknowledge that prayer is the only tool we have left.

My Friend, the Mover of Mountains

In remembering God's mercy towards us, it is helpful to remember the Three A's of God – *Authority*, *Abundance* and *Attention*. Let us begin by focussing on God's Authority. Yes, God is our loving Father. Yes, God is our dearest friend. Yet, he is also the Sovereign God of the Universe. The King of Kings. The Creator of Creators. He who fashioned the stars and made human life from dust. How wonderful is the moment we realise that He who has become our best friend is in control of the whole universe? He who writes our futures, loves us, and has our best interests in mind? There is a beautiful song that includes these lyrics: "When I lie awake and wonder what the future holds, help me to remember that you're in control." When we begin reading a new book written by an author that we know and love, we don't know how the book will end and yet we don't mind – we trust the hand of the master. How much more should we trust the Hand of the Master of all... Painter of every perfect sunset, Writer of true love stories, Sculptor who created lions, butterflies and giraffes! In my journey with Christ, my faith has been most strengthened by the moments God showed me His authority. I once struggled with a big problem for three years. I was in a deep, dark hole and in front of me was an

Abba Father

immovable mountain. I knew it was immovable because I had tried to lift it from every angle, in every way, for three long years. Finally, I admitted I couldn't carry it. I fell on my face before God, and I cried out: "God, I can't do this, only you can heal me." As crazy as it might sound, He did! God healed me. Two years later and that problem is now far behind me. I still have problems, but I have more hope. There is a bible verse I recently discovered, and when I first read it, I cried so many tears! Not only because I know it's true, but because I lived every letter:

> "I cried to the Lord with my voice and He heard me from His holy hill." – Psalm 3:4

Remember my friends, that your Loving Father has opened the eyes of the blind, permitted the paralytic to walk, healed the leper and raised Lazarus from the dead. It is with His authority that He loves you, and He will not hide His *grace* from those who seek Him with a humble heart! Pope Kyrillos VI, who was a saint, a man of prayer, and who tasted God's sweetness first-hand, tells us:

† thoughts †

The site of the Mokattam Miracle in Cairo, where God answered the prayers of Pope Abraam, St Simon the Tanner and the Copts by literally moving the Mokattam Mountain in the presence of Muslim Rulers!

"They looked to Him and were radiant, and their faces were not ashamed." – Psalm 34:5

Part 1 / My Friend, the Mover of Mountains

"Trust that God sees you. He hears you and feels for you, so your little matters are very big before His love and your big matters are very small before His might."

But how does this help us? How do we take this truth about God's wondrous authority, and apply it to our complicated and unsaintly lives? The answer is simple. Pray. Pray like you have never prayed before. Pray with tears, fasting and supplication. Pray about your Goliath – the stubborn sin that you cannot seem to overcome. Pray about your Red Sea – the impossible barrier you just cannot get past. Pray for a miracle. Pray for the impossible and watch He who fashioned man from dust, make miracles happen before your open eyes! For He is good, He is God, and He is Your Father!

Ask for Help, Receive Heaven!

Now that we are familiar with God's *Authority*, let us discuss God's *Abundance* – for it is truly a hidden treasure trove. When we consider that our faith requires our fragility, a constant repentance, a constant service and a constant love, it is easy to lose hope, for we blatantly fall short. We are "sinners", and what joy is there in being such a thing? The answer: dependence on God. Once we realise that we need Him – truly, need Him – we cry out to Him with our whole heart! For help, for grace, for mercy, for deliverance… and because He is merciful, He answers our prayer. Not only does He answer, but He answers abundantly. In fact, those who ask for help, receive heaven!

> "If God sees even a little true will, He provides abundant help for man, He sends His Grace in great abundance." –
> St Paisios of Mount Athos

Oh how wonderful it is to have your weeping turned into waiting and your fear turned into faith! Let us never tire of asking our Christ for help, especially in our times of dire need. What we will discover in time, is that He allows us to feel this deep need so that we accept dependence on His Mercy! Once we depend on Him,

Abba Father

we will discover the abundant treasure trove that God grants to those who humbly acknowledge their helplessness before Him who grants both help and heaven abundantly.

> "Find Jesus at the door of your heart and you will discover paradise." – St John Chrysostom

Let us unpack this. In difficult moments, we turn inwards; and if we turn inwards enough we may begin to consider the lowly state of our heart. Suddenly, we hear a knock and when we open the door we see the Lord, Jesus Christ! He is visiting you, asking to dine in the small home of your heart! Let our need be greater than our shame, let us invite Him in to heal and bless our hearts, and in His abundance – to crown our Spirits with the Paradise of Joy. Truly, *"the kingdom of heaven is within you."* (Luke 17:21). Let us open our doors gladly, knowing it was for this purpose that He came to earth, to save the sinners and not the righteous. Jesus is for you and me. Jesus is for the afflicted and addicted, the anxious and afraid, the uncertain and the doubtful, the lonely and the heartbroken.

> ✝ *thoughts* ✝
>
> When you are in strife, will you ask for help from He who will grant you heaven? Will you open the door of your heart to He who knocks, ever-so gently? In your eyes, your heart may be empty and embarrassing, but in His Eyes, it is an irreplaceable mansion He longs to live in. He calls out to you softly from the door: "Come to Me, all you who labor and are heavy laden, and I will give you rest." (Matthew 11:28)
>
> Can you hear Him?

God's abundant giving is His decorating and adorning the earth! For God could have simply created His earth to be mechanically

Part I / Ask for Help, Receive Heaven!

precise, as a Clock-maker might. Yet, in His kindness, He added an element of breathtaking beauty and mystery, adorning His good earth as only an Artist would.

> "Now if God so clothes the grass of the field, which today is, and tomorrow is thrown into the oven, will He not much more clothe you, O you of little faith?" – Matthew 6:30

Listen closely, God loves you! He knows you; He hears you; He accepts you and He is willing to give you Heaven! He is so eager in fact that He waits only for you to invite Him in, to ask Him for help.

He Never Looks Away

Here my beloved, let us turn our attention the final A of the Three A's of God – *Attention*. Do you know that at all times, you have the full and undivided attention of God? Do you know that He gazes fondly upon you, every moment of every day? Sure, when He sees you sin it hurts His Heart, but it could never mean He loves you any less – Jesus Christ loves you always. Too often in times of bitter crisis, we feel as though God has deserted us... This problem is so common to humankind, that Christ Himself once cried out: *"My God, My God, why have You forsaken Me?"* (Matthew 27:46) When we look to scripture for guidance, as we always should, we find something truly remarkable: God's reassurance that we have His undivided care and attention. Not only does God care about the big, eternal stuff, like our repentance and salvation, He also cares about the small stuff, like our food!

> **"Look at the birds of the air, for they neither sow nor reap nor gather into barns; yet your heavenly Father feeds them. Are you not of more value than they?"** – Matthew 6:26

Your clothing, your family, your relationships, and all your needs big and small, He will provide.

Abba Father

> "If then God so clothes the grass, which today is in the field and tomorrow is thrown into the oven, how much more will He clothe you, O you of little faith?" – Luke 12:28

Crazy, right? Sometimes, I wonder if there is any detail of our lives too small for God to care about. The Bible doesn't think so; it says even: *"the very hairs of your head are all numbered."* (Matthew 10:30). Beloved, if we know this *truth*, why don't we believe it? Maybe it is because when we suffer in trials and tribulations, we foolishly assume that God is punishing us? This is a silly, human idea. In fact, the very opposite is true: *"For whom the Lord loves He chastens."* (Hebrews 12:6)

> **"God has not forgotten the man to whom He sends suffering and trials, but in this way is providing His closeness to him." – St John Chrysostom**

† thoughts †

In front of every Coptic altar hangs an Ostrich egg. This reminds us that just as an Ostrich gazes constantly at her eggs until they hatch, so does God gaze constantly upon us, until we hatch into eternity! God loves us so tenderly. In Isaiah 49, He tells us: "Can a woman forget her nursing child, and not have compassion on the son of her womb? Surely they may forget, yet I will not forget you." Jesus' eyes are always on you...

Are your eyes always on Him?

What is the difference between one who experiences God's *attention* and *affection* in his trials and one who doesn't? Maybe it's faith. In a beautiful Coptic hymn called 'In the Midst of the Raging

Part I / He Never Looks Away

Sea', it says: *"And it seems that Christ has left me / But I no longer see Him because of my weak faith."*

Maybe we aren't experiencing God's comforting presence because of pride? For we know that: *"God resists the proud, but gives grace to the humble."* (James 4:6). This sentiment is echoed in another Coptic hymn: *"Help me lord, I want to lose myself in you / For my pride has blinded me from seeing you."* Ultimately, we must learn to surrender to God's cure, no matter how bitter the medicine He provides us is. Let us never be foolish enough to think that we are unloved by LOVE Himself!

Christ, the Hopeful Romantic

In the Western World, we often hear about 'hopeless romantics' – those who drift from relationship to relationship, seeking love and falling short. Too often we presume that all love must be like this – hopeless; a frail arrow tossed half-heartedly into the wind. This isn't true. Love: *"always hopes."* Jesus the Compassionate is a hopeful romantic. His love is eternal, and He never gives up on us. When we are confused and lost and we run away, He seeks us tenderly to bring us home again. When we shut Him out of our hearts, He doesn't leave. He waits and knocks softly, again and again. God loves us with that wild love, that love that goes beyond reason and limits. That love that hopes.

Sometimes we assume that God loves us the way that we show love, but God is perfect and loves us perfectly! He does not stop loving when He is abandoned, rejected, reviled, spat on, or shut out. See what a love like that does? It saves the world. God loves us with that Crucifixion love! That painful love. I know it is hard to accept this kindness, this grace, this LOVE – it's almost a gift too precious to claim. But it has your name written all over it, and God enjoys giving His beloved flowers too.

Abba Father

Let there be no doubts. God never gives up on us. God is never ashamed of us. God is never malicious towards us. We, who know our faults all too well, often flee when Christ comes to kiss our wounds tenderly. But we do not need to run, for we were created for this great Love. Do you want to know how deeply Christ desires you? He writes poems for you and proclaims them loudly: *"You have ravished my heart, My sister, my spouse; You have ravished my heart with one look of your eyes, With one link of your necklace."* (Song of Songs 4:9) Do you want to know how perfect YOU are in His eyes? Hear Him who cries out to you more truthfully than your shame and insecurities ever could: *"You are all fair, my love, And there is no spot in you."* (Song of Songs 4:7)

This Great Romance was never meant to be one-sided! For all great romances are reciprocated. Let us therefore love Him back with the love He fills our hearts with. Let us surrender to the tenderness of His touch; let us seek our Beloved from dawn till dusk – for He is our heart's desire, our only joy!

> **"The watchmen who go about the city found me; I said, "Have you seen the one I love?" Scarcely had I passed by them, When I found the one I love. I held him and would not let him go" - Song of Songs 3:3-4**

Sometimes, we too lose sight of Christ; and when we do, how do we respond? Do we also seek Him frantically, asking everyone if they have seen Him? Do we also refuse to rest until we find Him, and when we find Him – magnificent and smiling – do we cling to His body and refuse to let Him go? Do we also revel in His great love for us? Do we, like the Shulamite woman seek intimacy with our King? For she is not satisfied with seeking him in the open squares, but fondly speaks to Him, declaring: *"I am my beloved's, And his desire is toward me. Come, my beloved, Let us go forth to the field; Let us lodge in the villages."* (Song of Songs 7:10-11). Oh how sweet it is to love Him in private!

Part 1 / Christ, the Hopeful Romantic

Have we forgotten beloved, that *marriage* – the deepest love relationship available to us – was created by God to show us the relationship between Christ and the Church? Have we forgotten that all husbands ought to love in imitation of Christ himself – laying down their lives for their wives? For Christ, our Christ, is the Husband who will never give up on His bride. How often did Israel, His bride, turn her back on Him in stubborn disobedience? How often did she cheat on Him with false idols? Did she not, despite His perfect devotion – reject, ridicule and crucify Him as a criminal? And yet:

> "Father, forgive them, for they do not know what they do." – Luke 23:24

This is our Christ, the Hopeful Romantic. He is the Great Bridegroom, and we are His beloved Bride. Our Coptic Church has given us a beautiful liturgical hymn which we sing during weddings:

> *"Listen O bride and incline your ear, Forget your people and your father's house, For your chastity has appealed to the Bridegroom, For He is your husband and to Him you will submit."*

From this moment forward, I want you to promise me that you will not allow these words go in one ear and out the other. I want you to promise me that you will hold them ever-so tenderly, and treasure them in your inner Heart. For just as Christ loves us, and gave Himself for us, so that we could be sanctified and saved, so too are we His bride, and we ought to submit, to honour, to revere and to revel in the wonderful romance we share with the King of Kings – the Bridegroom, our Lord and Saviour Jesus Christ. Our God is good and He knows our humble abilities. He doesn't expect us to be perfect, He only desires that we surrender joyfully to this Great Romance of His! From this moment forth, let us not run from Him whom we know is good, kind, compassionate and loving.

Abba Father

† **thoughts** †

A beautiful illustration of the Beloved and her Groom, as found in the Song of Songs. Christ is represented in the shepherd and King. We, the Church, are represented in the Shulamite woman, who is called The Beloved. How wonderful it is to be called His beloved and pursued by The King! Truly, indeed: "we love Him because He first loved us." — 1 John 4:19

The Creator of Creators

How many of us who are artists, painters, musicians, and poets have ever realised that God is the Creator of Creators? This means that as creative people we have a special relationship with our Lord. King David wrote psalms and so did Moses – whose sister, Miriam sang songs! Noah created an Ark out of gopherwood, St Luke the Evangelist was a talented iconographer, St Paul of Tarsus and St John Chrysostom, as well as a myriad of other saints were gifted writers, preachers, and teachers. St Joseph was a carpenter, and as a boy Jesus Himself was a young carpenter too. Later in His life, we know that Jesus created wonderful, original parables and that He was a brilliant storyteller. But before all this, at the beginning of time, God the Father created the universe from nothing at all!

> "The earth was without form, and void; and darkness was on the face of the deep. And the Spirit of God was hovering over the face of the waters. Then God said, "Let there be light"; and there was light. And God saw the light, that it was good." – Genesis 1:2-4

Therefore, it is good and right to call God the Creator of Creators… For did not God call David, the simple poet, *"a man after My own heart."* (Acts 13:22)? And what did King David whom God likened

Abba Father

to Himself write about, but the wondrous creation of His Lord and Master? The Psalmist wrote:

> *"For You formed my inward parts; you covered me in my mother's womb. I will praise You, for I am fearfully and wonderfully made; marvellous are Your works" – Psalms 139:13-14*

God created *us*, and this is yet another reason to be thankful, for His creation is perfect, just as He is perfect! Thus, we can rest assured that our 'true selves' are never bad, ugly, incomplete or anything of the sort. When Christ lives in our hearts as He intended, we are perfect and whole.

> **"So God created man in His own image; in the image of God He created him; male and female He created them."**
> **– Genesis 1:27**

Why did God bestow upon us such a precious gift? Because He is a good, kind and faithful God!

> **"For we are His workmanship, created in Christ Jesus for good works, which God prepared beforehand that we should walk in them." – Ephesians 2:10**

Let us therefore walk in the ways that our Jesus walked. Let us also be storytellers, poets, writers, painters, iconographers, musicians, psalmists, songwriters and wood sculptors! For not only have such professions and paths been sanctified by the saints who walked in them before us; but it is God Himself who has granted us these creative abilities so that we might glorify Him!

> **"He has filled them with skill to do all manner of work of the engraver and the designer and the tapestry maker, in blue, purple, and scarlet thread, and fine linen, and of the weaver—those who do every work and those who design artistic works." – Exodus 35:35**

Part 1 / The Creator of Creators

✝ thoughts ✝

A Coptic Icon of the Creation of the World painted by UK Coptic Icons. This is a rare depiction and an extremely beautiful one. The next time you see a tree tenderly swaying or a seagull floating on the wind, will you glorify Him who made the birds to sing?

"O Lord, how manifold are Your works! In wisdom You have made them all. The earth is full of Your possessions." – Psalm 104:24

But what about those of us who don't enjoy making art? Those who prefer engineering and medicine? I say to you: blessed is your profession also, for Christ engineered the world and is the Good Doctor. Still, it is good to smell flowers, appreciate little things and express ourselves creatively. As a teacher I have found that everybody is deeply creative if they allow themselves to be creative… So have a go, and don't expect to make a masterpiece the first time around. All good things take time. Ruin a few pieces of paper, test out some ideas, and practice until you too can use your creativity to praise Him!

> "Take delight in all things that surround us. All things teach us and lead us to God. All things around us are droplets of the love of God—both things animate and

Abba Father

inanimate, the plants and the animals, the birds and the mountains, the sea and the sunset and the starry sky. They are little loves through which we attain to the great Love that is Christ. Flowers, for example, have their own grace: they teach us with their fragrance and with their magnificence. They speak to us of the love of God. They scatter their fragrance and their beauty on sinners and on the righteous. For a person to become a Christian he must have a poetic soul. He must become a poet. Christ

† thoughts †

An ancient Orthodox icon of the Theotokos, St Mary that is said to have been painted by St Luke the Evangelist. Some say this icon depicts her real facial features — how beautiful she is! Are you a painter? Why not paint an icon of your favourite saint for your prayer corner?

† thoughts †

A modern Orthodox icon of Saint David, the Prophet and King. I love this icon because it captures the poet's heart inside King David! Are you a talented poet, rapper or singer? Why not write God a love song, or sing a poetic prayer from the depths of your heart? Remember, God loved David's poetic heart!

Part 1 / The Creator of Creators

does not wish insensitive souls in His company. A Christian, albeit only when he loves, is a poet and lives amid poetry. Poetic hearts embrace love and sense it deeply." – St. Porphyrios

So, let us not only find God in His Church and on His altar, but in His clouds, in His sea, in His birds and His fish and His sunset and His stars and His giraffes and His little sons and daughters. Let us find God in the endless ocean and count His mercies with the grains of sand upon the earth. Let us smell His gifts in freshly baked bread and see His abundance in the tiny, fragrant flowers. Let us love Him in all His creation – the big and the small – that everywhere might become Heaven on earth. Finally, let us join Him in creation, that we might know and love Him more wonderfully.

Who We Are

At this point in the book, I would like to share with you some truths that will lift your spirits. These are God's promises about who you are after you put on Christ in Baptism. Remember, God's word is *always true*. I recommend reading these truths daily, each morning, for strength, hope and joy!

- ✞ I am beautiful to God - Isaiah 61:10
- ✞ I am blessed - Jer 17:7
- ✞ I am the salt of the earth - Matt 5:13
- ✞ I am the light of the world - Matt 5:14
- ✞ I am God's child - John 1:12
- ✞ I have eternal life - John 1:12
- ✞ I am Christ's friend - John 15: 15
- ✞ I am chosen to bear fruit - John 15:16
- ✞ I am forever free from condemnation - Rom 8: 1
- ✞ I am an heir of God - Rom 8:17
- ✞ I am a co-heir with Christ - Rom 8:17

Abba Father

- ✝ I cannot be separated from God's love - Rom 8:35
- ✝ I am gifted - Rom 12:16
- ✝ I am full of hope - Rom 15:13
- ✝ I am in Christ - I Cor 1:30
- ✝ I am a temple of the living God - I Cor 3:16
- ✝ I am bought with a price - I Cor 6:20
- ✝ I belong to God - I Cor 6:20
- ✝ I am a member of Christ's body - I Cor 12:27
- ✝ I am a new creation - II Cor 5:17
- ✝ I am a minister of reconciliation - II Cor 5:20
- ✝ I am God's co-worker - II Cor 6:1
- ✝ I am crucified with Christ - Gal 2:20
- ✝ I am alive in Christ - Gal 2:20
- ✝ I am a saint - Eph 1:1
- ✝ I am blessed with every spiritual blessing - Eph 1:3
- ✝ I am being saved - Eph 2:5-9
- ✝ I am seated with Christ in heavenly places - Eph 2:6
- ✝ I am God's workmanship - Eph 2:10
- ✝ I am becoming mature in Christ - Eph 4:13
- ✝ I am filled with the Spirit - Eph 5:18
- ✝ I am strong in the Lord - Eph 6:10
- ✝ I am empowered to obey God - Phil 2:13

Part I / Who We Are

- ✞ I can do all things through Christ who strengthens me - Phil 4:13
- ✞ I am honoured - II Tim 2:21
- ✞ I have a high priest who sympathises with me in all my weaknesses - Heb 4:15
- ✞ I can find grace and mercy to help in times of need - Heb 4:16
- ✞ I am holy - Heb 10:10
- ✞ I am a royal priest I Peter 2:9
- ✞ I am a partaker of the divine nature - II Peter 1:4

The King of Kindness

When I first came to know God and to see His magnificent presence in my life, I began to call Him by two different nicknames: the first was, "My rescue!" For so He was. The second was, "The King of Kindness." In my simple opinion, one of the most beautiful things about God must be His perfect kindness. We see this across the Bible: in Christ performing the miracle at the Wedding of Cana in Galilee for His mother's sake, in Christ rescuing the woman caught in adultery from the stones of the Pharisees, and in His simple love for small children, and the fact that He played with them... And yet, nowhere is God's kindness made as abundantly clear as it is in the Parable of the Prodigal Son.

Most of us are familiar with the story *(see Luke 15:11-32)*. A father has two sons, one of which asks him for his portion of the inheritance, *before* his father dies. Lovingly, the father complies. The prodigal son journeys to a distant land, wasting his father's money on sinful living... Ultimately, he winds up alone, starving and feeding swine. There, at rock bottom, the prodigal son finally returns to his senses! He decides to travel home at once, to beg his father for forgiveness and to hire him as a servant. Upon returning, his father greets him with overwhelming love, warmth, dignity, & honour.

Abba Father

> "Like the Prodigal Son, we must come to our senses." –
> St Paisios the Athonite

In order to understand this parable, let us begin by understanding the word 'prodigal.' The Cambridge dictionary defines being prodigal as: *"spending or using large amounts of money, time, energy, etc., especially in a way that is not very wise."* That means, in this context, that the prodigal son lived wastefully, in laziness and luxury – not honouring the value and dignity of his father's inheritance. How often do we too, who are blessed with the heavenly inheritance of love, rational thinking, intuition and authority, misuse such gifts in order to live wastefully and in arrogance? Nevertheless, we ought not to despair, for this parable teaches us that God's love is infinitely more powerful than our sins. The vastness of His heart is unfathomable to us. He can wipe us clean.

> "As a handful of sand is thrown into the ocean, so are the sins of all flesh as compared with the mind of God." –
> St. Isaac the Syrian

Let us once again, return to the parable to understand how God responds to us when we – heavenly dignitaries covered in the filth and dirt of sin – decide to humbly return home to the King's Palace and beseech Him for forgiveness. Does God say I told you so? Does God punish us? Does God passive-aggressively hint that this wouldn't have happened if we had just obeyed Him? No, God does none of these things, for God does not love us the way humans love, but the way that *only He can*.

> "And he arose and came to his father. But when he was still a great way off, his father saw him and had compassion, and ran and fell on his neck and kissed him." – Luke 15:20

The parable tells us that when the prodigal son *began* to return home, *before* he had even arrived, his Father – who represents God the Father, saw him and had compassion on him. This means that his Father was waiting at the door, looking out into the distance, longing for His child, hoping that he would come home again... Often in times like this I wonder how we could ever think God is cruel when He loves us so, with such a sweet, fatherly love? The following adage is true, God is good.

Not only was God waiting for him at the door, but when He saw His son returning home, with his head lowered, repeating to himself how sinful and unworthy he was, He *ran* to His son! You will ask, but why is it significant that He ran? In the 1st Century Middle East, running in public was considered shameful and unbecoming of an honourable man! The Father would have had to lift up His tunic and run through the streets – the equivalent of going outside in your boxers today – but God didn't care how he looked! He did not feel ashamed to love His broken son with an unconditional, Fatherly love! Imagine, the prodigal son walking home ashamed and cold, hoping only to be hired as a servant...

> **"But the father said to his servants, 'Bring out the best robe and put it on him, and put a ring on his hand and sandals on his feet. And bring the fatted calf here and kill it, and let us eat and be merry; for this my son was dead and is alive again; he was lost and is found.' And they began to be merry." – Luke 15:22-24**

Not only did the Father honour him as the Son of a King, as royalty. He also celebrated his change-of-heart by slaughtering the fatted calf, eating, drinking and being merry. This reveals to us the gladness of God and that heaven truly rejoices when we repent! More beautifully, however, it shows us how we should treat the broken, who are seeking God for the first time – as royalty returned!

The King of Kindness, in His mercy, does not only direct his kindness and compassion towards the prodigal son... The parable tells us that when His elder son returned home from tiling the field:

Abba Father

> *"... he was angry and would not go in. Therefore his father came out and pleaded with him."* – Luke 15:28

In the middle of the joyful party, the Father was not upset by the elder son's bitterness, nor concerned that he was 'killing the vibe.' Rather, He took the time to plead with him lovingly, explaining that he too was precious, and that He had placed His entire kingdom in his hands.

> **"And he said to him, 'Son, you are always with me, and all that I have is yours. It was right that we should make merry and be glad, for your brother was dead and is alive again, and was lost and is found.'"** – Luke 15:31-32

This message serves to comfort the seasoned Christians, that they might not resent the sinners whom God mercifully decides to shower in grace. That they should rather, celebrate the return of the broken, the lost and the weary into the loving arms of the Father. Knowing

† thoughts †

This painting is called 'The Return of the Prodigal Son' and was painted by the Dutch master, Rembrandt. It is considered by some to be his finest artistic work and one of the greatest paintings ever painted. I love it because of the Father's firm tenderness, the Prodigal Son's humbly repentant spirit and the humanity of the elder brother who is standing with his hands crossed. Let us praise the Loving Father and sing:

"Oh, give thanks to the Lord, for He is good! For His mercy endures forever."
– Psalms 136:1

Part 1 / The King of Kindness

His arms are wide enough to accommodate us all, and that as co-workers with Christ, all His Heavenly Gifts are ours – God does not withhold His Grace, His Mercy, His Peace, His Joy and His Love from His children! Rejoice with *all* therefore, knowing that no-one is neglected in the kingdom of the King of Kindness.

Jesus Loves the Children

The Holy Bible is full of astonishingly powerful passages that appeal to the child-like. These include: *"Blessed are the pure in heart, for they shall see God."* (Matt 5:8). As well as: *"give us this day our daily bread"*. (Matt 6:11). Those who choose to encounter God humbly and in simplicity know that these are more than words; the pure and simple truly see Christ with their eyes in every place. Did not God send St. Paul the Anchorite his 'daily bread' every day, that even in solitude he might be filled? And yet, of all the scriptures adored by the child-like, none cause rejoicing as much as this:

> "Then Jesus called a little child to Him, set him in the midst of them, and said, "Assuredly, I say to you, unless you are converted and become as little children, you will by no means enter the kingdom of heaven. Therefore whoever humbles himself as this little child is the greatest in the kingdom of heaven." – Mathew 18:2-4

From this passage we see that Jesus really loves children! He openly admits that they are the best. In this fallen world, most people value 'adult-thinking.' Mindsets and attitudes that coldly analyse people and situations: count costs, consider figures, invest wisely and chase success in a paycheck. But God, who sees all, prefers the little child – holding him up as the model of Christian perfection.

Abba Father

When Jesus' disciples got caught up thinking like 'adults', they asked Him which of the disciples would be 'the greatest' in the Kingdom of heaven. They wanted to be the best, as adults often do. What did Christ do? He brought an innocent child into their midst, to show them what greatness is.

> "And the child which He set in the midst I suppose to have been a very young child indeed, free from all these passions. For such a little child is free from pride and the mad desire of glory, and envy, and contentiousness, and all such passions, and having many virtues, simplicity, humility, unworldliness, prides itself upon none of them; which is a twofold severity of goodness; to have these things, and not to be puffed up about them." – St John Chrysostom

Why is the little child the greatest in the kingdom of heaven? His unconsidered virtue, his perfect humility, and most of all: his simplicity – the child does not plan or plot, but surrenders to God:

> "For children follow their father, love their mother, do not know how to wish ill on their neighbour, show no concern for wealth, are not proud, do not hate, do not lie, believe

✝ thoughts ✝

Fun Fact: The small child whom Jesus brought into the midst of the disciples as a model of perfection later became St Ignatius of Antioch, an early Church Father, who died as a martyr for Christ.

Just as our Gentle Jesus played with the children, He is willing to be our King and our Playmate!

"Delight yourself also in the Lord, and He shall give you the desires of yoru heart." - Psalm 37:4

Part I / Jesus Loves the Children

> *what has been said and hold what they hear as truth. And when we assume this habit and will in all the emotions, we are shown the passageway to the heavens. We must therefore return to the simplicity of children, because with it we shall embrace the beauty of the Lord's humility."*
> – St Hilary of Poitiers

Wise men have often remarked that when a child comes into this world, it is not time for parents to **teach**, but to **learn**, and Christ echoes this sentiment here. You who read these lines with youthful hearts – simple, pure, unassuming, hopeful, meek, optimistic and loving – blessed are your hearts! If I had the humility, I would sit and learn at your feet, for truthfully you are the very crown of heaven!

For those of us, who through the natural progression of life have drifted from our innocence, seeking wisdom, maturity, discernment, and wholeness – our search will ultimately lead us to where we began. Our destination is to become child-like once more, *in the awareness of our vulnerability*. It is easier for a child to view the world with unassuming simplicity, for he has not yet become painfully aware of evil, grief, betrayal, and toil – and yet, we whose hearts have been broken, must find the strength to trust again, knowing we may be stung and hurt, & by God's grace – loving anyway.

> "Therefore, beloved, the Lord instructs us that what they are by the gift of nature, we should become by the fear of God, a holy way of life and love of the heavenly kingdom; for unless we are alien to all sin just like children, we cannot come to the Saviour." – Epiphanius Scholasticus

For how could we dare approach the throne of the ever-patient God, aware of our wilfully committed sins and unbecoming deeds? Indeed, it is far better, to be like the small child; whom being told by His Father not to engage in a certain folly, obeys instantly, without investigating the instruction's intention. This is the small,

Abba Father

natural child's obedience to his earthly father. How much more ought we, the spiritual children of God, to obey our Heavenly Father whom we *know* does not lie? Jesus loves the children, this much we know. For when the disciples pridefully forbade children from approaching Jesus, Jesus rebuked the disciples and insisted that the children should come…

> *"But Jesus said, 'Let the little children come to Me, and do not forbid them; for of such is the kingdom of heaven.'" – Matthew 19:14*

Let these words caution us all, who in thinking like adults see ourselves as better and wiser than children, who laud age over the young and assure the youth they understand nothing. Let this chapter be a warning to all those whom in 'adult arrogance,' avoid playing with the children. Finally, to those who in wicked selfishness would abuse the finest and purest of God's elect, I remind you:

> *"But whoever causes one of these little ones who believe in Me to sin, it would be better for him if a millstone were hung around his neck, and he were drowned in the depth of the sea." – Matthew 18:6*

But now, let those who seek His Kingdom in simplicity rejoice, knowing that this humility is found also in The Heart of Christ. Simplicity is the path that Jesus esteemed most – the path of children. Let us then, like children, not only find God in the liturgy, in theology, in asceticism and in bitter struggle. Let us find Him also in joy, in play, in insects, in sunlight, in simply being. For God created us, loves us, and is truly within us! So much so that in our purest form, God shines through us!

> *"And now, little children, abide in Him, that when He appears, we may have confidence and not be ashamed before Him at His coming." – 1 John 2:28*

Remember Your First Love

You might think it odd that I am asking you to remember your first love… but I am not referring to the girl in pre-school that you thought was cute, I'm referring to your honeymoon with Jesus. Many of us, when we begin our Christian life, have one or more 'experiences' of God. This experience could be an answered prayer, a moment of indescribable joy, a big or a small miracle. Such moments are often called 'visitations of the Spirit,' but here I will refer to them as 'experiences.' St Paul had a colossal experience with God, where he was blinded by light, rebuked for persecuting Christ's children, and appointed to preach the gospel of God. In a moment, Saul became Paul; a murderer became an evangelist, and a tyrant became God's finest mouthpiece. I am certain that Paul, no matter where he went, never forgot this first encounter. St Peter's first experiences with Christ included Him healing his sick mother-in-law and filling his small boat with fish… I am certain that even unto death, Peter never forgot the *fullness* of his fishing boat. St Mary the Egyptian experienced God's grace when, after hearing her prayer for forgiveness, He allowed her to physically enter His Church in Jerusalem and instructed her on her path. St Anthony attended church on Sunday morning and heard this passage being read, *"If you would be perfect, go, sell what you possess and give it to the poor, and you will have treasure in heaven; and come follow Me"* (Mt.19:21). He promptly walked out of the church, sold all he had and pursued a life of monasticism – on the spot. What was it that drove all these wonderful saints to undertake such radical endeavours the moment they first tasted Christ? What did they see, hear or feel? Answer: Him, and simply put, they fell in love… They experienced Him, they loved Him and they sought Him forever.

Do you remember your first taste of God? For vulnerabilities sake' I will share some of my own. As a child, I had recurring, terrible nightmares that would only end peacefully when Jesus' face would enter my dreams. When I was around 9, I bought a hand-cross and walked around the Church joyfully that as a child I could hold and own such a blessed thing. Recently, I watched God move an impossible mountain for me, this experienced birthed and renewed my faith. I also experienced a moment where years of shame, insecurity and fear, faded, and I was full of love, joy and peace – this occurred directly after I had read the biblical promises of God for the first time! I will never forget these experiences and simply remembering them helps me fall in love with God all over again. I encourage you to reflect upon and remember the moments that Christ first touched your heart!

> **"Nevertheless I have this against you, that you have left your first love. Remember therefore from where you have fallen; repent and do the first works, or else I will come to you quickly and remove your lampstand from its place— unless you repent." – Revelation 2:4-5**

Time and time again, we are *unfaithful* to God – our Bridegroom. Biblically, our unfaithfulness is addressed in the book of Hosea, where Hosea's love and devotion to his unfaithful wife Gomer, symbolises God's unrelenting faithfulness to His adulterous bride – the people of Israel. When Moses was on top of Mount Sinai, the Israelites cheated on God by worshipping false idols. When

Part 1 / Remember Your First Love

St Peter was pressed, he denied Christ three times, in the Garden of Gethsemane the disciples whom Jesus loved couldn't even stay awake with Him to pray, in His moment of greatest need! There is no doubt that we have all, at times, been disloyal to God, and yet we *still hope*, for He is always faithful!

> "If we are faithless, He remains faithful; He cannot deny Himself." – 2 Timothy 2:13

God is truth, God is justice, God is love, and therefore, God cannot deny Himself. Thus, we can rest assured that despite our flimsy faith, our betrayals in times of weakness and our humiliating sins, Christ will never run away from us or forsake us. So why should we ever forsake Him? God's faithfulness to us is a wondrous promise indeed, as reassuring as it is redemptive. Christ's faithfulness to us is embodied by His own willingness to die a shameful death to save our souls!

> "...looking unto Jesus, the author and finisher of our faith, who for the joy that was set before Him endured the cross, despising the shame, and has sat down at the right hand of the throne of God." – Hebrews 12:2

St Athanasius the Apostolic, who is a champion of the Orthodox Church for the pivotal role he played in the formulation of the Nicene Creed ("We Believe in One God..."), wrote about God's faithfulness:

> *"Now the so-called gods of the Greeks, unworthy of the name, are faithful neither in their essence nor in their promises. They do not abide everywhere. The local deities come to nought in the course of time and undergo a natural dissolution.... But the God of all, being one really and indeed and true, is faithful, who is ever the same.... He is ever the same and unchanging, deceiving neither in his essence nor in his promise. As again says the apostle writing to the Thessalonians, "Faithful is he who calls you,*

Abba Father

who also will do it"; for in doing what he promises, he is faithful to his words. And he thus writes to the Hebrews as to the word's meaning "unchangeable": "If we believe not, yet he abides faithful; he cannot deny himself."

The hour is at hand and time is short, and we ought to remember the One who died for us. Not out of shame or fear or to preserve our souls, but because if we have ever *tasted* one iota of God's peace and joy, we know that nobody can touch us the way He touches us. Nobody smiles as beautifully as He smiles. No one embraces us as wholly and as warmly as He embraces us. Who else could love us with the perfect, sacrificial, and ever humble love of our Lord Jesus Christ?

† *thoughts* †

Do you remember the first time you walked into a Coptic Church, lit a small candle and tucked it softly into the metal box of sand before the icon at the door? Do you remember the moment you realised your little candle was a prayer heard in heaven? The moment you realised that the God of Heaven was your first love?

I urge you therefore to, *"Remember now your Creator in the days of your youth"* (Eccles 12:1). I encourage you to remember the visitations of the Spirit you have received; absorb them deeply when they come. Remember the miracles, the answered prayers,

Part 1 / Remember Your First Love

the mountains He moved for you. These doors you daily stroll through with ease, did you not once pray with tears they would open? Remember your hunger, your love, and your devotion. How when you tasted His Joy, you knew that nothing could ever take it from you, that nothing which opposed Him was worthwhile. Remember the intensity of your passion for Christ: the love letters you wrote for Him, the hymns you sung to Him from the depths of your soul, without any shame, for *"perfect love casts out fear."* (1 John 4:18). Remember your seasons of solid faith, the moments you KNEW that God was real. It is wise in seasons of spiritual joy and abundance to store up faith for the seasons of spiritual dryness.

> "Now in my prosperity I said, "I shall never be moved." Lord, by Your favour You have made my mountain stand strong; You hid Your face, and I was troubled." –
> Psalm 30:6-7

Part II
Prayer

"For prayer is nothing else than being on terms of friendship with God."
ST TERESA OF AVILA

Abba Father

"Ask, and it will be given to you; seek, and you will find; knock, and it will be opened to you. For everyone who asks receives, and he who seeks finds, and to him who knocks it will be opened." – Matthew 7:7-8

Part II / Protect and Preserve

Protect and Preserve

In these next few chapters, I would like to focus on knowing God through relying on Him in prayer. These chapters will only cover some of the many endowments we are able to ask God for. If you need these blessings, ask for them in prayer: *"Ask, and it will be given to you."* (Matthew 7:7). I know it doesn't always feel that way, but it really is that simple... Ask Him, and He will give to you. The first prayer I would like to encourage you to pray, is a prayer that God would *protect and preserve you.* Why should we pray for this? Because as Christians, we are soldiers of Light, Children of the True King, proclaiming His salvation to a world abound in darkness. Did Christ not warn us that as Christians we would be hated for His sake? However, in the same sentence He also said:

"But not a hair of your head shall be lost." – Luke 21:17-18

Oh, how wonderful He is! That He should protect our lives, our loved ones, our salvation – these alone would be an abundant grace. But our God is a God of details, and lavish love, and so He cares for *everything*. From our Eternal Life, all the way down to the preservation of the hairs on our head. As His children, we have a timeless weapon, His Word, which is a strong fortress during tribulations.

Abba Father

> "The words of the Lord are pure words, like silver tried in a furnace of earth, purified seven times. You shall keep them, O Lord, You shall preserve them from this generation forever." - Psalm 12:6-7

Have you ever wondered how on earth our humble selves are going to be Christians in such a difficult and unreceptive world? Fear not, for every generation has its own challenges, and the road to salvation is never easy, and yet God has considered your fears and promised you protection:

> "I will not be afraid of ten thousands of people who have set themselves against me all around. Arise, O Lord; save me, O my God! – Psalm 3:6-7

I have a dare for you. The next time it is late at night, and you are feeling hopeless, afraid, alone, overwhelmed and beset by evil on every side, find a picture of Jesus the Compassionate, or a cross, and put it on your pillow case. Ask for peace and sleep in the shade of Your Lord's *protection!*

> "He shall cover you with His feathers, and under His wings you shall take refuge." – Psalm 91:4

---

† thoughts †

As Christians we call the Holy Spirit 'The Comforter'... Remember that prayer is the best balm for your fears!

"May we all live in the peace that comes from You. May we journey towards Your city, sailing through the waters of sin untouched by the waves, borne tranquilly along by the Holy Spirit, Your Wisdom beyond all telling." – St Clement of Alexandria

Part II / Protect and Preserve

I do not say that all your troubles will disappear, for so long as we live on this earth, we will have no shortage of trouble. I say: your burden will be lighter, you will be protected, and even on your darkest nights, you will have access to indescribable peace & joy through your God who said to you:

> *"Peace I leave with you, My peace I give to you; not as the world gives do I give to you. Let not your heart be troubled, neither let it be afraid." – John 14:27*

Guide and Guard

The second prayer I encourage you to pray, especially in dire times when you feel that you are lost, is that God guides and guards you. As human beings, we grapple with a myriad weaknesses, doubts and fears which can create a cloud that obscures our vision – we're often partially blind. It is wise, therefore, to recognise that we need God's guidance to make good decisions, and we need Him to guard us in order to be safe. As we mentioned before, one form of guiding and guarding comes to us in the manner of scripture. When we keep His commandments, we are walking on an illuminated path to heaven, which the saints have walked before us. In short, we are safely shepherded to Him.

> "Every word of God is pure; He is a shield to those who put their trust in Him. – Proverbs 30:5

Are you about to embark on an important journey? Are you soon launching a business, starting a job, switching careers, getting married, having children, or seeking to heal deep wounds? This coming passage is for you – that you may remember that *God walks with you* & makes things work!

> "The Lord is your keeper; the Lord is your shade at your right hand. The sun shall not strike you by day, nor the moon by night." – Psalm 121:5-6

Abba Father

To those who feel that being protected from the burden of the day is too light a protection to serve you, I share with you a more comforting passage, that you may glorify Him in every circumstance:

> *"When you pass through the waters, I will be with you; and through the rivers, they shall not overflow you. When you walk through the fire, you shall not be burned, nor shall the flame scorch you." – Isaiah 43:2*

I know, that in periods of spiritual dryness, scripture can be experienced flatly, rather than coming alive in the heart. This flatness fades with the presence of the Holy Spirit, as strengthened by prayer, repentance, and communion. Rest assured, God's Word does not lie – but comes alive when we believe it in faith. For those of you who have not yet passed through raging waters, who have not yet walked through fire and remained unburnt; I will share with you the story of those who did.

In the Book of Daniel (Ch.3), we see that King Nebuchadnezzar of Babylon built a giant golden statue mandating that all the people in his kingdom must bow to the statue and worship it. The three saintly youth (Hananiah, Azariah and Mishael) refused to worship the idol and remained loyal to the God of Israel. As punishment for this, they were cast into a hot, fiery furnace! What happened next? *Christ Himself* in the form of a theophany (a pre-incarnate appearance) *walked with them* in the fiery furnace! He strengthened them so much, that they praised Him with a long and lovely hymn!

> *"But the angel of the Lord went down into the furnace to join Azariah and his companions, and shook off the fiery flame of the furnace. He made the inside of the furnace to be as though a dew-laden breeze were blowing through it, so the fire did not touch them at all, or cause them pain, or trouble them." – Daniel 3:49-50*

Part II / Guide and Guard

See how kind and gentle Our God is? That if he had stopped, or even eased their pain, it would have been enough. Instead, He caused it to feel as though a *cool breeze* was passing through the furnace. God's presence with them made that fiery furnace as comfy as an air-conditioned room! So often, we too feel like we're about to be suffocated by the smoke of exams, family problems, relationship turmoil and other pains, forgetting that Christ Himself is with us, *here*, in the fire.

> **"When the spirit is suffocated from inner turmoil and taken up with various kinds of restlessness, having been deprived for the moment of any hope of human aid and turning totally to the Lord, an angel of the Lord descends near to it." – St Jerome**

I love this quote by St Jerome because it reminds us of the power of prayer, and of this wonderful truth – that in our hardest times, especially when we feel all alone, God is more present than ever! You may know of the following tale already, but for our hearts' sake, I will share it again:

> *"One night I dreamed a dream.*
> *As I was walking along the beach with my Lord.*
> *Across the dark sky flashed scenes from my life.*
> *For each scene, I noticed two sets of footprints in the sand,*
> *One belonging to me and one to my Lord.*
>
> *After the last scene of my life flashed before me,*
> *I looked back at the footprints in the sand.*
> *I noticed that at many times along the path of my life,*
> *especially at the very lowest and saddest times,*
> *there was only one set of footprints.*
>
> *This really troubled me, so I asked the Lord about it.*
> *"Lord, you said once I decided to follow you,*
> *You'd walk with me all the way.*
> *But I noticed that during the saddest and most*

Abba Father

*troublesome times of my life,
there was only one set of footprints.
I don't understand why, when I needed You the most, You
would leave me."*

*He whispered, "My precious child, I love you and will
never leave you
Never, ever, during your trials and testings.
When you saw only one set of footprints,
It was then that I carried you."*

God is good, God is in control. He is your guide; He is your guard. Let us never forget that all that *is* and ever *was*, belongs to Him. Will they throw us in the fire? The fire obeys Him! Will they cast us in the sea? The sea parts for Him! Will they spit on us and curse us? They are His lost children! The more we see God in everything around us, remembering that not a hair can fall without His permission, the more we will feel comforted. God will never give you a battle too big for you. Oftentimes, He is simply trying to teach you to reach out to Him, to rely on Him, to live in Him. God permits our suffering for our own salvation, so let us not curse the day, but hope and trust and pray.

† thoughts †

In the Coptic Church, we honour the 'three saintly youth' in our Midnight Praises (3rd Hoos), when we glorify God in their words:

"Bless the Lord, O sun and moon, praise Him and exalt Him, above all forever / Bless the Lord, all you stars of heaven, praise Him and exalt Him, above all forever / Bless the Lord, O you rain and dew. Praise Him and exalt Him, above all forever."

Heal and Help

Another request I pray that you ask of God, that you might know He will not disappoint you, is that He heals and helps you. Across the Bible and the rich tradition of the Orthodox Church, God has helped & healed His people – in persecutions, in famine, in war and in every strife! Don't you know that if you cry out to heaven in brokenness, you are able to secure for yourself healing? Many wonderful examples of God's healing are found in the story of the Great-Martyr, St George. After being tortured horrendously and pierced with sharp knives, a voice from heaven was heard, saying: *"Fear not, George for I am with you."* A light shone, an angel appeared, and St George stood up – healed! Later, the emperor shod St George in iron sandals with red-hot nails in them, making him walk back to his cell. The next day, Diocletian asked him how he liked the shoes. St George, standing before the emperor with healed feet & a glorious sense of humour, said: *"they were just my size."*

> "What then shall we say to these things? If God is for us, who can be against us?" – Romans 8:31

During Jesus' earthly ministry, He spent most of His time healing those who were paralysed, blind, possessed, bleeding and even dead! Why? So we would know that *all* who turn to Him, despite

Abba Father

the extent of their deformity, can be restored to perfection in Life again. We must know that He who commanded death to return Lazarus, and who conquered death itself, can heal us in a *heartbeat*. Why won't we admit that we need a healer and a helper? Are we ashamed to be human and to rely on God? The paralytic knew he needed someone to help him enter the pool. Each day he begged that *anyone* would come and push him into the healing waters when they stirred, and each day he was disappointed. Then something happened that changed his life completely… He met Jesus.

> "When Jesus saw him lying there, and knew that he already had been in that condition a long time, He said to him, "Do you want to be made well?" The sick man answered Him, "Sir, I have no man to put me into the pool when the water is stirred up; but while I am coming, another steps down before me." Jesus said to him, "Rise, take up your bed and walk." And immediately the man was made well, took up his bed, and walked. – John 5:6-9

In this wonderful passage we find many spiritual pearls. Firstly, we find that in order to be made well, we must *want* to be made well – he who does not seek healing will not receive healing. Secondly, despite our thinking that our healing must occur in a certain way (as the paralytic thought his healing had to occur through the pool), our Lord Jesus Christ has his own ways of healing us. For by His Holy Word, nature was created, and at His Holy Voice, nature gladly conforms to His will. Finally, let us remember that to be healed we must have faith and be obedient, *always*. Could you imagine how silly the paralysed man must have felt when he was being told to rise, take up his bed and walk? The command defied all logic, everything he ever knew, and yet in faith, he did not delay.

> "Forthwith the sick man does as is bidden him, and by obedience and faith he gaineth to himself the thrice longed for grace." – St Cyril of Alexandria

Part II / Heal and Help

And what about Moses? His people were cornered at the Red Sea, beset by powerful enemies and facing certain death. With human eyes, Moses and the people of Israel were in an impossible situation. Yet, through the eyes of faith, Moses saw a different ending. He turned to his people and said: *"The Lord will fight for you, and you shall hold your peace."* (Exodus 14:14) Then he did what he knew could change the impossible, bend nature and save his people: he turned to God in prayer.

> **"And the Lord said to Moses, "Why do you cry to Me? Tell the children of Israel to go forward. But lift up your rod, and stretch out your hand over the sea and divide it. And the children of Israel shall go on dry ground through the midst of the sea." – Exodus 14:14-15**

There is a reason this story has been immortalised in Christianity. It is a testament to God's ability to do the impossible, to help those who cry out to Him in faith and to part our own 'Red Sea'. Therefore, let us remember that those who are doing good for the Glory of God are only ever one prayer away from The Power that parted the Red Sea, raised the dead and harrowed Hades!

I would like to share a gentle example of God helping us in all the details of our lives. When God created Adam and placed him in the Garden of Eden, God saw that Adam was alone. And in His infinite love and compassion, God was not indifferent to a man alone in paradise… God cared.

> **"And the Lord God said, "It is not good that man should be alone; I will make him a helper comparable to him."**
> **– Genesis 2:18**

God helped Adam by making for him a helper, and to this day, God helps every man who chooses the Holy Path of Marriage by making for him *his* helper and *his* equal, a friend to love and share Life with! I am certain that marriage is one of God's greatest and most

Abba Father

generous gifts to His people. To those who love Christ lonesome, He gifts a playmate and a friend, to till God's Holy Garden with.

> "Notice how the good God does not stop short, but adds kindness to kindness, and, in an abundance of riches, wants to clothe this rational being in every degree of esteem, and along with this esteem to regale him with a life of ease." – St John Chrysostom

So, the next time you are persecuted for your faith, ridiculed, mocked and bullied – I want you to remember the God of St George, who healed his wounds so effortlessly he could laugh about it. The next time you are obsessing over a solution for a problem, and you are stressed, anxious and alone, I want you to remember the paralytic whom Jesus decided to heal because of his simple faith. The next time you are in an impossible situation, with enemies closing in around you and unavoidable destruction looms over your loved ones, remember Moses; who reassured his people, prayed to God, and as a result, walked casually through an ocean parted in two. Finally, the next time you are lonely and wondering if God cares that you need a companion – remember Adam, whom even in paradise, God did not forget, but helped with a helper like himself. If you have needs, pray about them. We serve a beautiful God who He heals and helps all His children, for He is *truly* good!

---

† thoughts †

When God rescued the people of Israel by parting the Red Sea, Moses was so happy he sang a song of praise!

"I will sing to the Lord, for He has triumphed gloriously! The horse and its rider He has thrown into the sea! The Lord *is* my strength and song, and He has become my salvation; He *is* my God, and I will praise Him; my father's God, and I will exalt Him." – Exodus 15:1-2

Save and Sanctify

I urge you to pray that Jesus saves and sanctifies you, as well as your family, friends, neighbours, colleagues, and every other human being struggling on God's earth. Every single one of us needs someone to pray for us, to lift up our souls before the Lord. So today, let us lift up those who don't know God, before God – for if we do not pray for them, who else will? It is right and worthy to ask God to save and sanctify us, because it was for this *very* reason He was incarnated and became man. Jesus *died* so that we could *live*, and by His Grace, we no longer fear death. *"O Death, where is your sting?"* (1 Corinthians 15:55) Death, to the Christian, has become transformed into eternal life. Saint Peter, the rock, was saved from drowning in because he kept his eyes firmly fixed on Jesus, who permitted him to walk upon the water to reach Him. In *faith*, Peter walked…

> "And he said, Come. And when Peter came down out of the ship, he walked on the water, to go to Jesus. But when he saw the wind boisterous, he was afraid; and beginning to sink, he cried, saying, Lord, save me. And immediately Jesus stretched forth his hand, and caught him, and said unto him, O you of little faith, why did you doubt? And when they came into the ship, the wind ceased." –
> Matthew 14:29-32

Abba Father

Let us therefore, keep our eyes firmly fixed on Jesus. For when we pay attention to the howling winds of worry and the stormy seas of solving problems, we too will begin to sink in despair. We have a holy lighthouse in Christ Jesus! When we focus on Him, we too can walk on water, so to speak. St Peter was not the only one saved by faith in the One who called us to the impossible. St Moses the Strong, St Augustine, St Paul of Tarsus and St Mary the Egyptian were all saved and sanctified by the God who counted their broken hearts precious and set them on fire with His Holy Love. I encourage you in times of struggle to read their stories. They will remind you of God's saving grace towards us, that God wants YOUR heart – the broken, sinful, darkened and fearful one – to be His! Never forget that at Jesus' gracious touch, the Samaritan woman was made a prophetess, David – a king, Aaron – a priest, and Demas, the right-hand thief – the first saint to enter into paradise! So, ask Him who can do all things, to touch your heart with His grace and to sanctify you for His Feast.

> "For by grace you have been saved through faith, and that not of yourselves; it is the gift of God, 9 not of works, lest anyone should boast." – Ephesians 2:8-9

> "Thus also faith by itself, if it does not have works, is dead." – James 2:17

The above verses are very close to our hearts as Orthodox Christians when we discuss God saving and sanctifying us. They reveal two core tenets of our faith: the first being that we are saved by *grace* through *faith*, and the second, that faith without works *is* dead. If we remember these, we shall never be misled. There are some who will say that your actions have nothing to do with your entry to heaven, that faith is enough and grace fills the gaps. These people have forgotten one very important thing – that faith without works is dead. Therefore, let us who believe in the Living God, live our lives as a tapestry of good works, so that He may be glorified in us, and we may be glorified in Him. Let us remember however,

Part II / Save and Sanctify

that it is ultimately God's grace working in us that we rely upon to accomplish every good and noble deed – for there is no goodness at all outside of Jesus Christ.

> "Do not rely on your own efforts but on the grace of Christ. "You are," says the apostle, "saved by grace. Therefore it is not a matter of arrogance here but faith when we celebrate: We are accepted! This is not pride but devotion." – St Ambrose of Milan

Some of you who have perhaps forgotten God's loving-kindness towards us might ask, 'why would God want to save *us*?' I say in reply: why wouldn't a good God want the best for His children? Have you forgotten that God created us to live in paradise? In the liturgy of St Gregory, the priest prays:

> "Who for goodness alone, brought man into being from what was not. And You placed him in the paradise of joy."

In fact, the liturgy of St Gregory is full of wholesome and wonderful contemplations on the Loving God who not only saves and sanctifies us, but created us for His love, light and joy! It does not sit right with me to know of these magnificent words of and not share them with you:

> "You, as a Lover of mankind, created me, a man. You had no need of my servitude. Rather, it was me who was in need of Your lordship. Because of the multitude of Your compassions, You formed me when I had no being. You set up the sky for me as a ceiling. You made the earth firm for me so that I could walk on it. For my sake You bridled the sea. For my sake You have revealed the nature of the animals. You subdued everything under my feet. You did not permit me to lack anything from among the deeds of Your honour. You are He who formed me; And placed Your hand upon me. You wrote within me the image of Your authority; And placed within me the gift of speech.

Abba Father

You opened for me the paradise, for my delight; And gave me the learning of Your knowledge. You revealed to me the tree of life; And made known to me the thorn of death. One plant there was, from which You forbade me to eat. This of which You said to me: "From this only do not eat!" I ate of my own free will. I laid aside Your law by my own opinion. I neglected Your commandments. I brought upon myself the sentence of death."

This is how God loves us! Heaven is *for us*! Joy is *for us*! Life is *for us*! Light is for us! In fact, God who is perfect, does not even withhold Himself *from us*, but gives godliness to all those who seek Him with their whole hearts. As Coptic Christians, we are called to be sanctified by God's grace and our own toil. We are called to be restored to the illumined image and likeness of God, in this earthly lifetime. In theology, this process is called 'deification'. Deification refers to the process of becoming more *like* God through His grace or 'divine energies.' We never become God, but people see God in us, because the more we let Him work through us, the more His Love radiates through our smiles.

> "Historically, deification has often been illustrated by the example of a sword in fire. A steel sword is thrust into a hot fire until the sword takes on a red glow. The energy of the fire interpenetrates the sword. The sword never becomes fire, but it picks up the properties of fire." – The Orthodox Study Bible

Therefore, let us pray for the salvation and sanctification of both ourselves and the world. For God in His loving-kindness towards men, is willing not only to save us all, but to make us shine with *Him*.

> "as his divine power has given to us all things that pertain to life and godliness, through the knowledge of Him who called us by glory and virtue, by which have been given to us exceedingly great and precious promises, that through

Part II / Save and Sanctify

these you may be partakers of the divine nature, having escaped the corruption that is in the world through lust."
— 1 Peter: 3-4

† thoughts †

Another word for 'deification' is 'theosis.' This is an Orthodox icon of the theosis of the saints with Christ. See how they shine with the same light and glory? This is the gift that God gives those who love Him!

Bless and Beautify

Finally, I exhort you to pray that our Lord Jesus Christ bless and beautify your soul, your heart, your mind and your spirit – the entire totality of your being. For He is capable and willing to bless you with *every* good thing, and to beautify your heavenly heart from every earthly blemish.

> "And God is able to make all grace abound toward you, that you, always having all sufficiency in all things, may have an abundance for every good work." – 2 Corinthians 9:8

We must always remain connected to the loving presence of our Abba Father, who longs to lavish every good thing upon us. This remembrance will allow us to constantly turn to God in prayer, trusting that He cares for our big problems, small wishes, and unique dreams. He longs to bless your path and to make all things well for you, He longs to bless you with the unique desires of your heart.

> "Blessed is every one who fears the Lord, who walks in His ways. When you eat the labor of your hands, you shall be happy, and it shall be well with you. Your wife shall be like a fruitful vine in the very heart of your house, your children like olive plants all around your table. Behold, thus shall the man be blessed who fears the Lord. The

Abba Father

> Lord bless you out of Zion, and may you see the good of Jerusalem all the days of your life. Yes, may you see your children's children. Peace be upon Israel!" – Psalm 128

Not only does Christ bless those who ask Him pure-heartedly with their material, physical and psychological needs, Christ also longs to bless us with a deeper, *spiritual fullness*. Have you ever tasted stillness in the middle of a storm? Perfect peace in the heart of an avalanche? Ask of Him who gives to all in abundance and without measure, for He is capable of sweetening your sorrows.

> "But the fruit of the Spirit is love, joy, peace, longsuffering, kindness, goodness, faithfulness, gentleness, self-control. Against such there is no law." – Galatians 5:22-23

You might ask, 'Why does Christ yearn to bless us with every gift?' I say, He loves you, with all His heart. You are His chosen bride, and He desires that you shine, spotless, at the Great Wedding Feast. For when you love someone, don't you desire for them – light, joy, peace, and every form of fullness?

> "that He might sanctify and cleanse her with the washing of water by the word, that He might present her to Himself a glorious church, not having spot or wrinkle or any such thing, but that she should be holy and without blemish."
> – Ephesians 5:26-27

God is good, and His desires are good! Therefore, He does not desire for us to be lost and suffering in the shadow of death, in constant anxiety, bent over with bad posture and no hope in Him! God desires that we be beautified slowly into His perfect image and likeness, by walking in The Spirit.

Part II / Bless and Beautify

> "The perfect will of God is that the soul be changed by reverence, having been brought to the full flower of its beauty by the grace of the Spirit, which attends to the sufferings of the person who undergoes the change." –
> St Gregory of Nyssa

Therefore, let us not worry and complain when we are tried and tested. In truth, we are being perfected. Is not gold and every precious metal purified in a fiery furnace? Is it not that young royalty, even on earth, are prepared vigorously for the responsibilities of the throne? So too must we, who hope to one day stand without shame in the presence of God and His saints, be purified through sufferings, trials, & tribulations. Let us then rejoice in difficulties, knowing that we are being prepared as a Bride is prepared for her Groom – lest we attend our own wedding in rags. It is much better to surrender joyfully to whatever medicines Christ has prescribed, no matter how bitter.

> "For it is absurd to be grateful to doctors who give us bitter and unpleasant medicines to cure our bodies, and yet to be ungrateful to God for what appears to us to be harsh, not grasping that all we encounter is for our benefit and in accordance with His providence. For knowledge of God and faith in Him is the salvation and perfection of the soul." – St Anthony the Great

How can we, who are weak and prone to error, be prepared to stand *shamelessly* in the presence of God? We can do so through transformation, which requires God's grace in abundance, as well as our own efforts. We must be prepared to leave behind our sinful ways to align our hearts with His.

> "And be not conformed to this world: but be transformed by the renewing of your mind, that you may prove what is that good, and acceptable, and perfect, will of God." –
> Romans 12:2

Abba Father

> "Those who are moved... to turn again to the Lord out of that state of deformity wherein worldly desires conformed them to this world must receive from the Lord their reformation." – St Augustine of Hippo

Do not fear, have you forgotten that God is good? He will not test you *"beyond what you are able."* (1 Corinthians 10:13) God is love. He is not a bad-tempered teacher just waiting for you to stumble so He can cast you into hell – that is not God, that is not good, and that is not LOVE! God is eternally *on your side* and He has equipped you for this journey! He has given you promises as a post-card from your destination, scriptures as a trusty map, the church fathers as an experienced guide, an Orthodox Church as a ship sailing directly to heaven, and a mobile phone called prayer – lest you need to call your Loving Father at any point, and for any reason at all. God will help you.

> "For the LORD takes pleasure in his people: he will beautify the meek with salvation." – Psalm 149:4

I am reminded now of a beautiful hymn we often sing after the Liturgy on Sundays. It is full of consoling words for you, God's chosen saints, on your journey home to the Heavenly Jerusalem.

> *"O seeker to meet Jesus / forget your hunger and thirst / Your food is the bread of life / and you'll drink from His wounded side. / You traveller forget the past / and you'll go steadfast in the path / if you suffer on the road, remember for you He died. / The trumpets will be heard soon / with happiness and sound of joy / a great feast above the clouds / and a crown for the watchful. / He'll prepare a place for you / He's always waiting for you / His heart is longing for you / blessed are you if you are prepared / You are part in Jesus Christ / you who live among the rocks / have no fears from all dangers / you're protected by the Lord."* – O Seeker

Part II / Bless and Beautify

† thoughts †

As Christians, we are all on a journey to heaven, so travel we must. However, we decide whether this journey is a terrible ordeal or a joyous hike through the forests of God's loving-kindnesses. Which path will you choose?

"You will keep him in perfect peace, whose mind is stayed on you: because he trusts in you." – Isaiah 26:3

www.ingramcontent.com/pod-product-compliance
Lightning Source LLC
LaVergne TN
LVHW091315080426
835510LV00007B/502